MODERN POETRY

For The Estranged And Forlorn
(Includes LGBT Poems)

By D.S. Barton

 **FriesenPress**

Suite 300 - 990 Fort St
Victoria, BC, Canada, V8V 3K2
www.friesenpress.com

Copyright © 2014 by D.S. Barton
First Edition — 2014

ISBN
978-1-4602-5486-8 (Hardcover)
978-1-4602-5487-5 (Paperback)
978-1-4602-5488-2 (eBook)

1. Self-Help, Motivational

Distributed to the trade by The Ingram Book Company

MODERN
POETRY

UNIQUE

I don't see you as a loser
I hate that word
I can't see you as less
As though you're
Second or third
At times when you're down
It leaves me sad

I need you to know
There is nothing bad
In any way about you
You have my heart
That will always be true
Whether near or apart
Your goodness shines through

You have my love and respect
For all that you are
Your determination and drive
Will take you far
So special and kind
With a sensitive mind
Not weird, just shy
Unique and sublime

TRUE FRIEND

People love you a lot
There's no in-between
I must admit
You're an interesting being
You've been the best friend
I've ever known
You know who I am
And still won't disown

You're the best company
When I'm feeling blue
God only knows
What I'd do without you
Your loyalty and kindness
Always provides
The understanding
I need inside

You accept me
As I am
And always show care
Your consideration and love
Have no compare
You are my true friend.

BRAVE

You show so much strength
In the face of terror
You charge right in
With more courage
Than error

Your love for your country
Has no compare
Whenever you're needed
You will be there

Your comrades
Will trust you
Through thick
And through thin
Your unselfish bravery
Will lead you to win.

MISS YOU

I miss you so much
Your sweet, tender touch
No one can replace
Your kindness and grace
The sound of your voice
That smile on your face

I have been blessed
To have you
Share my space
You were my
Soft place to fall
I'll always recall
The love that we shared
And how much you cared
I miss you.

BULLIES

Bullies are the very worst
They seem to have
A nasty thirst
Please don't let them
Choose me first
As they start
My lips are pursed
Seems as though
They're well rehearsed

To disappear
Would be the best
And finally lose
This repugnant pest
They harm
The innocent at will
Ensure there's no place
Left to fill
Try to keep
You feeling small
Thinking there's
No hope at all

Bullies are the very worst
Leave you feeling
You've been cursed
The life you have
Is worth much more
Than awful deeds
And words can score.

BE KIND

It's easy to be mean
And cause a big scene
It takes care to be kind
And relieve someone's mind

A compliment can go far
To calm a painful scar
Make someone feel good
Act the way you should

Put away the barbs and daggers
Be kind to a person that staggers
Take no heed of obnoxious braggarts
No need to grovel
Or act like beggars

Showing compassion
Can change one's reaction
Make someone gleam like a treasure
So they can look forward with pleasure
To a life beyond measure

DISMISSED

I have been dismissed
So much
That I'm pissed!
Repudiated and placed
In a subpar space
They won't be content
'Til I'm gone
With no trace

Deaf ears
Reject my case
To ensure
I have no base
The only voices heard
Are malicious and absurd

DADDY

What a difference
Life would be
If you had lived
To be there for me

The unsaid I love you's
And absence of hugs
The long talks were missing
That make you feel loved

Living devoid
Of your guidance and love
No protection
From bullies and thugs
Mistreated and used
Self worth abused and
Ground in the dust
Concealing the hurt
Became the main thrust

Walking around
Feeling empty inside
Most of the time
Just wishing I'd died

There was no one but mom
To give a care
Or acknowledge
My grief anywhere
You would have seen and cared
Shown us that love
Is much better shared
Not to be hoarded between two
But better spread out
Amongst a few

Words left unspoken
Can leave one heart broken
Lonely and lost
They came at a great cost
I didn't see
That you would be
The greatest loss
Of all to me.

ESTRANGED

It can be so hard to love yourself
And treat yourself as you should
When everyone who's been in your life
Treats you like you're no good

They bark and they bite
Hold on to spite
Provide no support of a positive kind
Staunchly entrenched in one state of mind
Using anything they can find
Ensuring that you're always maligned

Manipulate and control is the method applied
Sure to hold onto their pernicious pride
Never letting past issues subside
Stirring the pot, all involvement denied

DO I?

Do I apologize for being?
Or do I walk away?
Should I blame myself for not seeing?
Enveloped in all this grey

Do I recognize others are worse off?
It's obvious to me
Deprived of the solace
They so clearly seek

Do I fear love's gone forever?
As the past grows distant in mind
Do I regret the errs most remembered?
The results seem clarified

Do I remember the way that you loved me?
And made my heart satisfied
Do I forgive myself past indiscretions?
Or punish myself for all time?

Do I look forward to the future with pleasure?
Finally leaving the hatred behind

CRUCIFY

Some people love to crucify
They never let a chance go by
To belittle and bash
Make you feel like trash
With a twinkle in their eye

Speculation and gossip at the fore
They never cease to come back for more
Pound and pound
Never let up
On this type of fodder
They hungrily sup

It never dawns
The person they hate
Now has a damaged heart
Due to their prate

They have no good hand
In the person's fate
Made sure she knew
She didn't equate

Go merrily along
Your self-righteous path
Crucifying
While spewing your wrath

GET BACK

Get back
'Cause you don't know me
You can't see me
Only as a target
For derision and disdain

I can't count the times
I've had to refrain
From speaking the words
I've wanted to say
Wanting you to stop
Treating me as prey
Leave me in peace
Stay in your fray

The accusations
Attacks and blunders
That never cease
Make me wonder
If it was someone you loved
Would there be such thunder?

The disparaging treatment
Stays in my head
Making me dread
Time spent in your stead

PERFECT

Some people believe they're perfect
And always look down their nose
Ostracizing those they deem lesser
Their cynical will imposed
Designating those they consider best
Writing off the ones viewed as failing the test

They group together to revile and smear
To revel in their bonding
As they continue to sneer
Complacently content about
The failure they know
Confident she'll never grow
Satisfied with the status quo

Sometimes the cast-off is far more
Than some ever see
The easy choice is to ignore
The person they could be

If there's no forgiveness in your heart
Don't complain 'cause we remain apart
Nobody is perfect, each of us has faults
There's no excuse for pretense
Or one-sided assaults

When you always judge the exterior
And never look inside
You can miss the soul of that person
And their goodness is belied

RACIST

Your prejudice is plain to see
When you're in the vicinity
The snide comments and churlish looks
Your impish grin is all it took
For me to see just what you are
You're racist

The hateful words you utter
No longer make me shudder
I should have known
It's all home grown
Ignorance
Family did condone
Taught from birth
Color of skin implies less worth

When hatred is recited again and again
Eventually it's bound to sink in
You believe you're not
But when put on the spot
It's clear what you are
You're racist

Those who are racist
Will never concede
One little bit
The true reason why

They remain in a snit
Perhaps it's because
They'll never admit
Just what they are
They're racist!

KIND

I thought you were kind
Boy, was I wrong
I was totally blind
And now I so long
For a kind word or gesture
That comes from the heart
I'm cold and alone
Where can I go?
To find the warmth
That I crave so

PERPLEXED

I don't understand you
That much is clear
The way that you act
When no one is near
The insults you shout
The hurt that you spread
I admit I'm perplexed
Can't get in your head
So I'll back away fast
Leave you in the past
I'm perplexed but I'm done
You won't be the one

SAD

I feel blue when I'm around you
Your putdowns are a clue
I need to be true
To who I am too
Learn to wade through
This mire of goo

I am sad
Tired of feeling bad
Longing to be glad
To be free of you
Will be a dream come true
So I can move on anew
With a clear, fresh view
And stop feeling sad
'Cause I fell for you

GOOD RIDDANCE

There was a time
When you'd scream in my face
Call me out of my name
So often I'd brace
For the onslaught to come
For weeks at a time
All of a sudden
You'd turn on a dime

You made our lives hell
That is the truth
You'd never admit
Or acknowledge abuse

Your words were a weapon
That filled me with dread
Aimed to harm
And mess with my head

Hope you get yourself together
Stop denying your truth
Recognize your faults
And mature from your youth

I'm so glad it's over
And that we are through
Go on with your life
And good riddance to you

FEAR

Fear isn't real
It's all in your head
It paralyzes
And fills you with dread
Leaves your potential tossed aside
Missing experiences that
 Fill you with pride

Fearful, anxious
Bereft of confidence
Don't let those feelings
Have control or providence
Ignore them completely
Pass on by
Never give up
Reach for the sky

NAYSAYERS

The naysayers thump
The naysayers bash
The naysayers want you to
Stumble and crash
They want you to fall
And surely to fail
Just to ensure
You're kept low on the scale

So low that bottom is all you can see
So low you're blinded by darkness beneath
When you glimpse the light
Zoom in and head to it
Leave the naysayers behind
Believe you can do it

They want to keep you small
Far beneath them all
So you can't stand tall
Climb up over that wall
Stay strong not to fall
Listen up, hear the call
This is no time to stall
Strive to be who you are
The best form shown so far

Hold that dream, grip on tight
Move straight on with all your might
Keep the life you want in sight
When dreams come true
The world opens to you
So step right up, receive your due
You're more than those who block your view
You deserve something good and true
To prove yourself to those you knew
All along
Were wrong about you

NEGATIVITY

Negativity seeps like venom into a gash
Makes bitter souls slander and bash
Haughty and horrible
Quick to lash out
Stifling tensions swirling about

Put downs spill out swift and steady
Don't know how to begin to get ready
Any signifigance crassly denied
Uncontained hubris leaves many snide

Not permitted a thought or to speak your mind
Some ideas cut off midstream
Are more important than they seem
No chance to speak of your dream

HIGH AND MIGHTY

It's a long peer down
From high up on your perch
I 'm so far beneath you
You may have to search
Forever the victor
You'd never lose
Confident you'd win
And do as you choose

Your subjects are many
And all will condone
That you are the winner
And that you have shown
You're above most anyone
That you've ever known
Your ego is huge
Your pride is great
No matter who's harmed
They're discarded as waste
How mighty you must feel
To never mistake
Regardless who's left
To contend with the ache

MASTER AND SERF

You mock and scoff
I wish you'd back off
Stay out of my face
Quit obscuring my space
Stop trying to replace
Ignore and erase

Totally obstinate and intertwined
Toxic, haughty and narrow of mind
Leave me be
'Cause you're way too blind
To recognize others
Can see you're awry

Take your judgments and shove them
'Cause I know you're no gem
Rigid and rude
Sarcastic and crude
Fake and so phony
You're full of baloney

Drag along your minion
That has no opinion
She knows no other way
Than be sure to obey
For the master that owns her
The serf will always succor

No brain full of thought
For she has been bought
Completely controlled
She does as she's told

THE GREATEST LOSS OF ALL

When I was six years old, my dad passed on. I don't use the term passed away, since I noticed my friend Michelle, who has lost her father, some siblings and friends, says passed on. I like that much better because it's gentler and less heart-wrenching than the term passed away.

I realize now, all the positive traits that girls who grew up with dads, assume and take for granted, that I've never experienced. They have confidence in themselves and their own ideas and goals. It was the only solid relationship I would have ever been a part of with a loving man. It would have been great to be "princess," just once while young or feel special in a positive way. To experience the self-esteem and self worth I never had or possessed. To feel the love and warmth I had felt when young and my dad held me on his knee while sharing his dish of mom's rice pudding with me. I lost out on everything, the hugs, the outings, the long talks, being made to feel included or worthy of anything, minus the acid-tongued comments and disapproving grimaces.

The only love I've ever known came from my mom. Besides my dad, she's the only person who really did love me. I know because my siblings did everything they could to try and make sure she wouldn't love me. It didn't work because she did love me, even if they didn't. My estranged siblings have real love for each other. I can't figure out what to do with all their hatred for me. Where do I put it all? I've decided to hand it over to God, rather than contemplating suicide. Eventually I had to realize and accept that I would never belong there because I have no place amongst them. The only love my sisters have is for each other and their own. Now they've completely excluded my family from Christmas as well. I am the outsider, always have been. Born too late to a family where I wasn't really wanted or loved enough to be included properly. I was more of an irritant and nuisance than anything else.

I was made aware while I was young, that my parents and siblings had wanted a boy, not another girl. They had bonded as siblings for ten years before I was born. I was totally in the way. I was never supposed to be part of the plan. When I was young, I was so naïve that I believed I would rate the same love they had for each other. What a fool I was to think they would have some feelings of love somewhere in their hearts for me. I was the intruder. They were never going to embrace me with any real love. All my life they've been saying that I was the reason for the problems in the family. I came into that family as a baby. How am I to blame for their resentments against me? What about from birth to age fifteen? Even I'll admit I was quite a nightmare as a teenager. I was angry, alone and depressed with no real siblings to talk to or have positive communications with and no real hope for the future. I was always by myself in my bedroom. If they had just once, thought of putting their selfish resentments aside and actually shown me some love instead of making a point to berate and shove me aside. Maybe I wouldn't have grown up feeling like an only child, with no siblings that gave a damn or wanted me around.

My niece Treena was the closest thing to a sister I had growing up because she lived with us most of the time back then. I didn't appreciate how good a person she was either. She is the sweetest person ever and is the most like mom of anybody in the family. She has great qualities and a huge, kind heart. She's the best, just like mom was and I love and miss her. I wish Treena was my sister. At least then I'd have one. I stay away because all my sisters ever needed are each other, that's always been extremely obvious to

31

me. Growing up, my siblings gave me next to no protection, no advice, nothing to help me understand that I mattered too. As a person I mattered. I knew I didn't. My sisters' love fest with each other continues to this day. I've known lots of families with three sisters. I never saw one sister excluded while the other two meant the absolute world to each other. The constant exclusion is very hurtful and thoughtless. I accept the way they are because it is what it is.

It's the way it's always been and always will be. They come first and so does their relationship. It must be terrific to know you're special enough to be loved unconditionally just the way you are without judgments and a huge heap of biases stacked against you from the onset. Can they even imagine how they would feel if they never had that person attached to them throughout life that will always love and accept them as they are? No! When it comes to being selfish, I learned from the best. I always knew that once mom was gone that would be the end and it was. She was the only person in my whole life that actually did love me. Mom always included me and tried to make me feel like a part of the family. Even though there was always one of them badgering her about me or should I say against me? It's awful with mom gone, the love left with her. There's no love from anyplace but my children and my good friend, Michelle. The difference from my siblings is, mom loved all of us. She didn't pick and choose who she loved more and exclude the rest. We all mattered, not just the favorites.

My siblings love to proclaim that I got here alone. It's not their fault, they were never involved. I was all on my own. Those words are true, I must confess. They in no way helped me become my best. That gift is only given to the people they truly love and care about. I've never been on that list. Abandonment and ridicule can't give a person security and good self-esteem. It actually strips you of any confidence you may have acquired. Those are the times

I would have gone to my dad, to get the advice I never had. His comfort and love would have meant so much. Going through life without a dad has made me see just how very important having a father is, especially a good loving dad.

When I finally got up the nerve to tell my sister Alice that my dream was to become a writer, she feigned interest and care. Not one word of sincere encouragement or support, as usual. After they dissected my dream with each other, she of course replied by mocking my hopes and dreams for the future, with negative comments and sarcasm. She even laughed at me. That's all they've ever done, belittle and treat me like I'm ridiculous and have no value as a person. I've written a few children's stories that I'd love to have made into books. My sisters have never read one word I've written. Probably because they aren't fair enough to give an unbiased response. I now realize, it doesn't matter one iota what their opinion is at all. It's tainted as far as I'm concerned. They can give their opinions to each other, as they always have. I have to believe in myself. For the first time ever, I do. When no one at all believes in you, it's best to focus on your dream more than ever.

Many people in this world don't have family. They have to make a family of their own with good friends and those who love them. People they're comfortable being around. That's clearly what I must do. Stay away from those who enjoy my failures and won't let go of their hatred. When I was a teenager I was thoughtless and selfish. I didn't appreciate how great my mom was or how very lucky I was to have her at all. She was the sweetest and best person I was ever going to know. Mom was never vindictive or unkind. She was a beautiful person. I will always love and miss her. No one at all can compare to her. One of my sisters is fond of saying that I wasn't there for mom when she was in declining health. The reason I didn't come around much was because mom was at her house. I didn't like going to her house because it felt like walking into a trap. Super uncomfortable!

Here is one of many accusations made against me by Brenda when mom stayed there. It was mom's birthday in the late '90s and very hot and muggy outside. The only reason I went at all was because it was mom's birthday, so I took my girls with me. Something kept telling me to stay home that day. I should have listened. When it comes to me, Brenda is very big on accusations, pointing her finger and using reproach and indignation as a weapon. We were in the living room speaking with different people. After awhile we went to sit with mom in her room. I should have left the door open or looked out into the hall because after awhile we heard lots of footsteps outside mom's door. If I had looked out I would have seen the person who had been in the hall and went into Brenda's room. Later, when we get home, I get a phone call from mom asking me if I took $20. from a family friend, Louise's purse. I had already made a point previously to stay away from Brenda's room because she always accused me of stealing. I never went near her room that day. I already knew to stay away or be singled out. I was nowhere near anyone else's things. When I called back to talk to Brenda, she started screaming at me over the phone, accusing me of taking the $20. from Aunt Louise's purse. She said it could have only been me because everyone else there was a Christian and they wouldn't steal, it had to be me. Next, she got on the phone with my brother. Then his wife Rochelle calls mom and insists that she confront and accuse me as well. Oh yeah, I forgot to mention that Brenda found the $20. in her own dresser drawer and then accused me of putting it back.

I was angry at myself because if I had just looked into the hallway while we were in mom's room I would have seen the person who really stole the money. There was no point in calling my brother because he instantly defends Brenda, no matter what. He wouldn't have listened to a word I said regardless. It hurt so much to have them all attack me and not once consider there were many other people in her house. They were judge and jury and I was convicted with zero proof, for something I never did, by people who were supposed to be family. People that hate me so much they couldn't wait to point fingers and put their paltry two cents in. I believe the situation was karma for past misdeeds but that doesn't make them right for all being against me.

They treat me like I'm nothing and then they're surprised that I grew up feeling like I'm nothing. What I would like to know is why nothing was done to help me when I was young. Anyone with a brain could see I had very real issues with anxiety and depression, especially after daddy died.

If I had a counselor or someone to speak with, that could have made a huge difference in my life. I didn't have the bond or support they all had with each other. Maybe then I wouldn't have gone through life feeling like I was a mistake that shouldn't have been born and didn't belong anyplace. They had each other, they had no use for me. I should have stayed away from Brenda from then on. I always knew she had it in for me. She's always made rude, backhanded remarks to me. She always made me feel inferior to her. I was always fully aware that Alice was the preferred sister. Brenda never wanted me around. I still remember being a teenager and sitting at the top of the stairs listening to Brenda downstairs badmouthing me to mom. She would freak out and start yelling at mom, always about me. Once I asked mom why I was always the focus of her rants. Mom didn't know what to say. Brenda was like a missile locked onto her target. There was a time when I called mom mama for awhile. I stopped because Brenda was so offended by me calling her mama that she asked mom in an angry voice, "Why does she keep calling you that?" What was mom supposed to say? Because I'm her mother too. She never really liked me and resented me from day one. The same goes for my brother Robert, who vomited when I was born because I wasn't a boy. What a heart-warming story that was to grow up with. It's a very discouraging feeling knowing you were unwanted from the day you were born.

Brenda is always protected and always will be. The very same people that would never defend me at all, would fall over themselves to defend her. She could say or do anything and get away with it, especially if it refers to me. How nice it must be to have real siblings that love you no matter what. That's unconditional love. I'll never know anything about that. Brenda dashes my spirits and leaves me feeling worthless. It would be more honest if they just admitted they never wanted me in their family. The thing with Brenda and Alice is that they always return with another attack and more allegations from over 30 years ago.

There are two more allegations that I want to address. Brenda keeps accusing me about a ring of hers I stole when I was 15 years old. This took place so long ago that I don't recall who has it. This person apparently approached them with the ring still on her finger after 35 years. They accuse me and then refuse to tell me who has the ring. Whoever it is, she sure was in no hurry to give it back. It's not like Brenda couldn't be found. If this person felt so bad having her ring, she obviously never tried to give it back. The third and most ludicrous accusation, is that I stole their old wedding dresses from the '60s and '70s, which were in a crumpled old box in the cubby hole in mom's house. When mom cleared out the cubby hole, she probably threw out the old box. They both accused me of selling them.

They're so intent on blaming me for anything and everything they can come up with. What would I want with their old wedding dresses? They were too old-fashioned anyway and none of my friends would be interested at all. That's when I knew they were never going to stop treating me this way. They can't help themselves. That's why they talk down to me and enjoy mocking and laughing at my ideas. They're toxic and mean.

Also, my brother doesn't know the reason why my oldest daughter never visited him and his family is due to the fact that my meddling sisters insisted I not send her there. They said, "Oh no! You're not sending her there. He's too bossy and controlling."

They insisted I not send her. So, I never did. They also didn't want me to send my daughter Samantha to be in my nephew Stace's wedding. I would have let Samantha go if it hadn't been for Robert's hateful attitude toward me over the phone. If I had known my sister-in-law Rochelle was terminally ill, I would have definitely let Sammi be a part of Stace's wedding. They all knew Rochelle was sick and said nothing to us. They always want to make sure that I come off as the one who's uncaring and hateful, while they control things from behind the scenes as always. What none of them seem to recognize is, how hard it is to send my child to be with people that can't manage to have a normal conversation with me, even over the phone. None of them would do it. I also realize it's futile for me to ever make any attempt to reach my brother because he will always hate and reject me, so I won't. I learned long ago to just stay away, so that's what I do.

Once my book is published, I would like to read other life stories from people who come from families that leave them feeling isolated, unwanted and hopeless due to 'relatives' who want to eternally judge and punish them for regretful things they did or didn't do in the distant past. Those people who enjoy throwing past issues in their face repeatedly. No sign of forgiveness or releasing past resentments. Making sure they never let you forget you did wrong. These are the exact same people that would never tolerate anyone doing the same to them and would never treat those they love so poorly.

My sisters never admit to anything they determine in their private bubble that would make them look bad. The saddest part is, my daughter Denai loves many of the same things as my brother Robert, spicy food, nature and she adores watching sports, all sports, especially hockey, football, basketball, soccer and tennis. If he didn't hate me so much for the past, they could have been very close, instead of strangers. He would have been a good uncle. All my sisters ever wanted was to be in charge of the whole family, on their own terms. Now it's all theirs. They have exactly what they've always wanted, complete control. I've been shut out for decades. Now I'm gone. I hope they're finally satisfied. They won, they all won. They've always wanted me gone, now I am. I accept that I will never fit in or belong around them, I never did. I never felt good enough to even be related to them.

That's what my book is about. How I've felt all my life, as an interloper in that family. I now realize that the greatest loss of all has affected everyone's lives, mine and my children's. I had no dad and no grandparents. The care and wisdom came straight from mom. She already had her hands full because each of us had our own needful ways. The only thing my siblings have taught me about love is that it's completely conditional, especially when there is none. I never knew what I wanted to become. A while back, I finally figured it out. I had been writing all my life. That's it, write. When I was 16, my mom told me that my dad had wanted to become a writer. Why didn't I know right then? How could I not know? I didn't know because I was all alone. I didn't know because all my siblings ever did was point out what was wrong with me.

They've ignored me for most of my life and then they all sit back to criticize and judge. That's one thing they're all expert at, judgment. How well would they have turned out if they had gone through all their worst times alone with nobody to talk to or anyone to help them out or give advice and guidance. They all had each other for all those years while I was being bullied and mis-treated on a daily basis. Where were they then? If I never have to see my brother's hate-filled glare at me again, it will be too soon. My friend thinks their hatred for me comes so easily because they were so disappointed that I was born at all. I messed up their group of three. When people want you gone, you can feel it. They're hypocrites to so easily shun a quarter of the family, while they're all love and good wishes to everyone else. If they wanted us to know just how much we are the outcasts, it worked. My daugh-ter said not to bother with people who dislike me because she wouldn't give them a second thought and she wouldn't shed a tear over them. If they want to hold on to hatred for me then let them but I refuse to be burdened by it anymore. All I want is to write poetry and children's books for the rest of my days, find some joy, steer clear of the haters, stay close with my own and don't go where I don't belong. All I want are true friends I can value for the rest of my life and to veer far away from those who are fake, hateful and contrived.

Anytime I've entrusted either of my sisters with anything personal, they talk over me, regurgitate my words between each other and then turn around and use my words against me. I don't trust them and won't again. Everything is done for show with them. They think they are supreme judges of everyone and everything as they remain concealed in their comfortable bubble, where they control every minute detail. They keep making comments about my childhood, as though they lived it. They don't know me and never did.

They were nowhere to be found when I was a child. Alice was always in the U.S. marrying her latest dysfunctional husband. Brenda spent 12 years traveling back and forth to Grand Forks Air Force Base most every weekend, hoping to land one of many G.I.s. They were never around. Now, I am intent on surrounding myself with the people who do love me, or at least like me somewhat. You can't force anyone to love you. They either do or they don't. You can certainly tell when you aren't loved. I now know, above everything else, I needed my dad. I needed his warmth and love throughout my life. I needed his guidance, protection and strength. All the special gifts bestowed by a father who loves his daughter. What I didn't need was the frosty silence, cruel insults or the physical assaults by my brother Robert, who has hated me for as long as I can recall. I needed their love, not more damage to my self-esteem.

My siblings had daddy for sixteen years. I only had him for six years, neither is enough time. All the blanks and abandonment would have been filled in for me. If only he had lived. He was the greatest loss of all in my life. He was the empty, lost part that was never complete. I now see that I have to complete this journey by myself. Try to fill in all those empty blanks. I am grateful to God for giving me the knowledge to create, express myself and finish my book. The past three years writing my book has been like much needed therapy for me. I'm trying to understand myself and my past. Fill in the spaces that were never filled in. Trying to figure out why these people loathe me instead of love me. Why do they hate me so much? Those are the times I feel like dying. Trying to reconcile and understand the depth of their angst for me. Those are the times I speak to Jesus because it hurts so much and I can't bother others with my pain.

All I have to say to those who turned their backs to me is, for the first time in my life I get to have my say and the right to my own voice without interruption or being disregarded, as though I have no value or the right to be heard. No one deserves a life sentence for past mistakes. I didn't kill anyone and don't deserve to be judged and persecuted by anyone, for the rest of my days. Going through this has made me recognize how fortunate people are who have pure pasts, haven't done anything wrong and don't harbor any serious regrets due to their past. How their spirit must soar and what a guilt free existence they must live.

QUESTIONS

For a very long time, I've had some questions for Christians. I want to be clear, some of the best and some of the worst people I've known or encountered are Christians. My mother and my sweet aunts, Cleo Whiley and Viola Marsman, belonged in the absolute best category. They were funny, loving and kind, with a dry wit that runs through the whole family. Why do so many Christians act superior, snarky, unfriendly and love to exclude anyone different from them? If you believe in God so strongly, why do you judge others so much and act like it's your right to do so. Shouldn't you all be handing your judgments over to God? Many of you have closed minds and are superficial, gossipy, shallow and very haughty. They can be so unkind and unwelcoming. I want to become a Christian because I realize that I matter too and so does my soul. Every life matters, all humans matter. Don't hide your light . Let it shine, shine, shine. Let it shine! Despite what those who dislike me, think or say. Jesus loves me and I love Jesus too. That's the problem with having low self-esteem. Always thinking you're less and unworthy of anything special.

I DON'T CARE

I don't care what you think
I don't care what you do
Believe it or not
 I wouldn't want to be you

You're abrasive and mean
So critical it's obscene
Controlling and austere
You've made it quite clear
I don't belong near

Far away I will stay
It's much better that way
Stand clear of the path
Of one who bears so much wrath
No more glaring looks
You're one for the books
Keep your judgments
You hold so dear
No wonder I can't stand to be near

It does appear
Your greatest fear
Is to look in the mirror
And have to admit
You're a two-faced hypocrite
That enjoys berating
The family misfit

WORDS THAT MATTER

I've waited for someone
With words that matter
Not aiming to hurt
Spurn or shatter
No need at all
To bruise or batter

A person that's smart
Has a good heart
Can tell you feel small
And see past the wall
You've built to protect
Yourself from them all

A person with insight
Who'll detect your plight
Encourage you to acquire
The confidence and might
Help calm the anxiety and
Advance with more fight
Teach the things
You were never told
How to get past
The issues of old

DEAR JESUS

Thank you for forgiving my sins
Your love is where my life begins
Knowing you're here to protect me from hate
Means more to me than I can state
Surrounded by haters
No forgiveness in sight
Has made me see that you are the light

So, thank you dear Jesus
For all of your love
You are definitely sent
From heaven above
I thought my life was over
Now I see it's just begun
Because of you I can see the sun

Your blessings are so many
Never dreamt I would get any
My soul wasn't worth a penny
'Til you came into my life

Thank you dear Jesus
For showing me the way
Out of darkness
To see a brighter day

Couldn't find forgiveness
Or any place to start
Suddenly yours was there to have
The weight lifting from my heart

All I can say is
Thank you Jesus
Thank you dear Jesus
For giving me
The chance to see
All are precious in your grace
Each are given a special place

UNWELCOME

One of the things I liked best about Whitney Houston, was not only her great voice. It was her love and enjoyment of going to church. I never enjoyed going to church ever. I was forced to go almost every Sunday since I was around five years old. Some of the kids in Sunday school were unbelievably cruel and mean. There was this one big group of kids, all related, who made Sundays unbearable. They would all group together in a clique and treat me and my friend Fay like crap. They laughed at us, taunted us, insulted us, called us names and endlessly mocked and snickered behind our backs and to our faces in church.

They were the kind of kids that really enjoyed making us feel awful about ourselves. No one ever made them stop or shut up. Their bad behavior was permitted to continue, even during church service for a decade. What really turned me off was watching those same rotten acting bullies all run to get baptized. When I saw them do that , it was the last thing I wanted to do. They were the last people I ever wanted to emulate. That's why to this day, I disagree with children being baptized when they're too young to know anything. While they're too young to know anything about empathy, respect, kindness or how to treat other individuals decently. When I was about fourteen years old, I refused to go back to church. To this day, I'm uncomfortable and unenthused about attending church due to the awful way I was treated. I had to rebel to get out of going there anymore and to get away from those nasty, mean bullies. After that, I got labeled "bad." It was assumed so much that I was bad, so I started behaving badly. I figured, they're all accusing me of being bad all the time, I might as well be bad.

And I was bad. I stole things and was as dishonest and selfish, as the day is long. Due to my past, I've been accused of things I've never done. I've been accused for things that took place over three decades ago. Talk about holding a grudge forever! All I know is, I caused more harm to myself and my good, sweet mother, than anyone else. To this day, I still feel greatly disliked by both Christians and family alike. I'm sorry to those who feel materially harmed by me in the past. I was lost and damaged inside and no one did a thing to seriously help me. I was completely alone and abandoned by people that should have loved and protected me. Instead, they threw me to the wolves and left me there.

When my oldest daughter Denai was about ten years old, I let my sister Brenda start taking her to Sunday school at the same church, until Denai told me she was being mistreated as well. There was no way I was going to let the same damage happen to her, so I kept her home once she started experiencing the same bullying. When I saw that look in her eyes, like her self-esteem was waning, I never sent her back there. Interestingly enough, it was some of the children of those same people that had bullied me, that were treating my daughter the same mean-spirited way. You can bet they're all Christians too. If you don't know how to treat others decently then you're too young to be baptized. It's like some sick joke that prevents good kids from wanting to know the Lord.

I've been completely lost for most of my life. No father since I was young, to give me the confidence, knowledge and strength of character I needed. To teach me follow through, self-respect and respect for others. I grew up feeling isolated, anxious, angry and shy with no self-esteem or confidence in myself. Unwelcome and unwanted. If I had been given more useful advice and solid encouragement with fewer putdowns and condemnations, things may have been different for all of us.

HEART OF GOLD

A heart of gold is a great treasure
So rare to see
It imparts much pleasure
Warms your soul
Makes you feel whole
Gives you hope
That life will get better
Like receiving a special letter

For your eyes only
You won't feel lonely
When this love warms you
From head to toes
It will help to ease your woes
Be sure this special person knows
A place in your heart steadily grows

In this place you see their face
Be grateful for this sacred find
This blessing is one of a kind
Whose glow will soothe your troubled mind

A PLACE OF MY OWN

I would love to have a place of my own
Somewhere to go where love is shown
A place to reflect and feel whole
To contemplate, breathe
And call my home
Where I am free
To live and roam

BEST FRIEND YET

Some calm would be great
To wash over my mind
Some peace and cheer
Would be a welcome find
Just put on some tunes
And drift away
Laugh with a friend
And rehash the day

Kick back and groove
You've nothing to prove
Better yet
Hold your pet
The only unconditional love
Some ever get

Their unbreakable loyalty
Leaves no regret
No need for concern
To worry or fret
A loving pet is the best outlet
For that extra love they need to get

Anyone who owns a pet knows
Love for them continuously grows
They're adorable and sweet
Best buddy you could meet
Your special pet
Is the best friend yet

HEAVEN SENT

You are the one I've longed to see
Who has flitted in and out of my dreams

From time to time throughout my life
I've dreamt of you on lonely nights

To have you here
Your voice so near
Touch your face
Melt in your embrace

I thank God for you and know dreams come true
'Cause I will share my life with you
You are heaven sent

LGBT POEM (Don't Do It.)

Don't do it.
Give yourself the chance to grow
In mind and thought learn as you go
A worthy person to the end
Many hardships to contend
Find your path and start a trend
Follow through right to the end

Special in your very own way
Give yourself the time to say
I'm sure that I do want to stay
Live to greet another day
Know that you will find a way
To show that you are more than fey

Don't do it.
Know with time the hurt will fade
Enjoy the memories that you've made
With loved ones that are steadfast and staid
Have no need to revile or degrade

As time goes on life will improve
Do what you're meant to, make a move
Proceed ahead, find your groove
Many doubters to disprove
Know your value
See that you've
Come a long way
To be the authentic you

Don't do it.
You're worth much more
Life has good things in store
Just for you to go explore
Set your sights high
Soar through the sky
You'll see when you try
The answers to why
You're here become clear
Like God's whispering in your ear
You're here to overcome
Prejudice and jeers

QUEER FOLK

Queer people are some of the most unique, vibrant, interesting, fun, uplifting, friendly and creative people anyone could ever hope to meet. All the forms of discrimination they face has made many of them insightful, caring and confident in themselves as worthwhile human beings. It seems they gain strength and vigor from the adversities and various adversaries they've encountered. Instead of feeling bad about who they are, they have gay pride to pave their way and a great outlook on life. That makes them very special indeed. In a world filled with hate, greed, ignorance, apathy, cruelty and rejection, to name a few. Queer folk seem more optimistic, content and happier in their own skin than many people seem to be. A huge positive is, they take no heed of what haters think or say. That has to be more freeing for your soul than ingesting every hateful word shouted by homophobes with tiny, closed minds. People with humanity who aren't afraid to be themselves are cool with me. Queer folk seem that way to me.

SMALL DUMB AND MEAN

Small are the minds
Too jaded to see
Homophobia and bias
Far too extreme

Dumb is the intolerance
Harbored there
Shunning good people
With so little care

Mean are the hearts
That create despair
The hostility and rancor
Carried there

God and Jesus
Mere mortals not
Have infinite vision
Beyond our lot

Wiser than those
Who use any excuse
To discriminate and
Fling verbal abuse

WOUNDED

God is here for everyone
Not exclusively just for some
We all have pain and wounds are deep
So much that it makes some weep

Even though the hill is steep
Keep plodding on until you reap
The benefits that you deserve
And own a peace you can preserve

In time you'll learn to block the pain
Peaceful thoughts will calm your brain
You'll realize you're not insane

Think a good thought
Shout your name
Know that you are
Not to blame
Release your stranglehold on shame

SORRY, GOD

So many screwed up people
Attach themselves to you
When in truth
They haven't got a clue
Haughty and mean
They sure are keen
To twist your story
And snatch your glory

Nobody's born with a broken soul
Souls are broken along the way
No one should be defined
By the lowest valleys in life
That's an unfair price to pay

So, sorry God
For all the haters
That scoff and mock
And are forsakers

OBLIVIOUS

The sardonic cackle of laughter
Rings in my ears
A familiar sound I've dreaded
All these years

It meant you don't belong here
Get out of the way
We must speak in private
And you cannot stay

Knowing you're nothing
Inflames all your fears
The really bad times
Always ended in tears

A huge disconnection
That leaves you adrift
No one who's willing
To make forgiveness the gift
Blind to your agony
No arms outstretched
Leaves you feeling
Abandoned and wretched

No one understands
Or cares to know
How bad you're feeling or
How low spirits can go

Always on guard
From the snakes that hiss
Knowing I'm someone
No one would miss
'Cause they are all oblivious

HUMAN

When you aren't allowed to be human
What judgments you face
Others that make the same mistakes
Are pardoned without disgrace
None of the criticisms thrown at you
Are ever tossed at them
'Cause they are loved and protected
Too precious to condemn

Everything is theirs to have
Nothing is too much
While you and yours are valued less
Painted by a tainted brush
Every special date ignored
Encouragement withheld
Spread to those who matter most
The cherished make out well

Manipulation becomes an art
When it's all you have to impart
Fool me once, but twice? No way!
Nevermore to be led astray
Though not a favorite, I'll adjust
My major mistake was giving you trust

I may not be perfect
I am human as well
There were numerous times
When I stumbled and fell
I stayed down when I should have got up
Not seeing how much I would disrupt
I'm weary of this place
On the bottom rungs of the ladder

I want to ascend up and away
From the disheartening critics
With too much to say
Get to where it just doesn't matter
Far away from all the loud chatter
Too busy finding myself
To let nonsense shatter

Out to meet new allies solid and deep
From which positivity tends to seep
            Those wise enough to see beyond the wall
Who won't respond with anger and gall
People with empathy that proceed with tact
Far removed from negative impact

Those with good hearts and compassion to spare
Who let you know others have also been there
            People with insight who see past the blight
Those able to listen and console without dissin

Encouraging words can only help when you're low
Support can provide a good place to go
A flicker of humanity would not go amiss
Some long lost recognition would prove hard to resist

When you're lost and alone
Estranged and forlorn
Fallible and imperfect
Just human,
        No reject.

OUTCAST

Being pushed aside
Can make you hide
You don't go outside
'Cause you stayed in and cried
Feeling as though there's nowhere to go
To heal your hurt or mend your woe

When the people around you
Provide no support
It seems some relationships
You should abort

Be done with the strife
Move on with your life
Then judgments and criticism
Won't stab like a knife

Some things that are broken
Cannot be fixed
When you're the outcast
Your viewpoint is nixed

When the whole family is mentioned
And you're the ones left out
The fact that you're the outcasts
Leaves no doubt

JUDGMENTAL

The weight of judgment can be so strong
It seems as though you're always wrong

Naysayers will imply
You'll fail
Even when you try

What they don't know
What they don't see
As they try to diminish me

I am smart and
I am kind
Too much scrutiny
Makes some blind
Too critical
To ever change their mind

It's easy to mock and disavow
Those who should be held dear now

INSECURITY

Insecurity makes some pander and pant
Leaves them weakened and looking scant
Desperately coaxing and trying to connect
With someone, anyone
They meet or detect

Seeming lost and out of control
Acting in ways that detract from the soul
Removed from their character and far from the goal
Of making themselves healed and whole
It gets to the point where shallow types flee
To abscond from their vicinity
Take a good look inside, improve the flaws
That left you deflated and lacking good cause

LOVED V. LOATHED

When you are treated with favor and care
You can do anything, go anywhere
The support means so much
The love carries you far
Helps you know who you truly are

When love is withheld
And disparagement reigns
It leaves a huge hole
Filled with all kinds of pain
The judgments are harsh
The language is cruel
The wall is so high
There's no sun to view

The pain inside sears
It brings you to tears
While being shut out
There is lots of doubt

When you don't belong
Much can go wrong
The knives in your back
Can make you attack

STATE OF MIND

My state of mind is not so good
Been with me since my childhood
Through it all I have withstood
That gaping void called sisterhood
No one to speak with who gives a care
Not really wanted anywhere

Suffering from depression since very young
A target of the mean-spirited
And those with an acid tongue
Thoughts of ending my life
Came with great pain that stung
That's no longer an option I'm glad to say
Jesus has shown me a better way

Ignored and shunned
Lonely and stunned
My state of mind is not so good
Will find my way through
And become understood

LATE BLOOMER

I'm a late bloomer
Wish I'd realized sooner
Never did fit in
With many of my kin
Never felt like I belonged
Not once forgiven
By those thought wronged

Accusations turned to attacks
Answers kept in a secret cache
Answers so special they cannot be told
Answers so cloistered
They've schemed to withhold

Stories supplied with their very own end
Twisted to fit a disparaging trend
Conjoined sisters that pretend
Their preference for each other does extend
To those they exclude and condescend

Having two sisters that act as one
Feels so lonely when all's said and done
The end result is, may as well have none

I'm a late bloomer, ten years too late
Couldn't catch up, no matter the date

THINKING FORWARD

The human condition is churning
It seems as though too few are learning
They cannot contain their yearning
As their wants and desires keep burning
Exact same outcomes recurring

All of you are in clear view
The petty instigators too
Those who act hateful
Should really be grateful
Those who act mean
All believing they've seen
The person you've been
Meanwhile in-between
You've grown from just green

Continue thinking forward
Don't fall back
Enough time wasted
Focused on the wrong track
An enormous heap of anguish
Will impede those who languish

I'm closing the book
On that chapter of life
Leaving behind those
Who bask in my strife

YOU DON'T KNOW MY PAIN

You don't know my pain
So don't act as if you do
Very pretentious
And eager to impugn
You're convinced
You know my childhood
But you don't have a clue
Your arrogance makes me angry
My response is overdue

The damage wrought by bullies
Left scarring deep inside
Made me avoid your oppression
And harsh, excessive pride

Denying that you've had affect
Really turns me off
All your life you've held the reins
And had subjective thought

Your attitude left me deserted
Inferior and distraught
Always on the outside
Denied an inclusive spot

Don't assume you know me
And have it all figured out
Your gravest error was thinking
I had nothing to offer as clout

To have my dream dissected
And raked over the coals
Will never make me give up
Or abandon any goals

Each of us has our own story
And I have mine as well
The fact that you despise me
Doesn't make mine less to tell

TRUE WILL

Leave the past to hold your sorrow
Know there is a brighter tomorrow
You deserve your happiness
No need to feel that you are less

Those who love you always will
All through your life and even 'til
You shine a light on your true will

YOUR VOICE

You have the right to your own voice
To speak of things that are your choice
Don't be dejected, ignored or shunned
When you speak out some will be stunned

Come right up, have your say
Finally, this is your own day
Know your mind, keep it clear
Before you know it
Your time will be here

EPILOGUE

KEEP GOING

When no one is on your side
Keep going
Hold your head up
Keep going
Don't let the skeptics tear you down
Keep going
Keep your eyes on the prize
Keep going
When nobody is supportive
Keep going
Though doubted and dismissed
Keep going
Listen to your inner voice
Keep going
When your spirits start to drop and confidence wanes
Keep going
Believe in yourself more than ever
Keep going
Pray for guidance to get past bad times
Keep going
Until your dreams come true
Keep going.

BEAUTIFUL MAN

(This poem is dedicated to
President Barack Obama
 because he truly is a beautiful man.)
4.22.13

Intelligent and warm
The focus of much scorn
A good decent man
That does what he can
Constantly reaching out
The target of prejudice
 And paranoid doubt
       While the haters
Scheme, lie and pout

Loving his country
Doing his best
To fix the calamities
Dumped in his path
While thwarted opponents
Attack with great wrath

Disgruntled adversaries
Dig in their heels
Taking no heed
Of what the public feels
Fairness and reason

Discarded with haste
Leaving the destitute
Ignored with distaste
Thinking they're superior
And nobody sees
What they're all up to
Or how hateful
Some can be

A beautiful man
With his soul intact
Who doesn't let the onslaught
Deter or detract
From the person he is
Distinguished with grace
Who more than deserves
His prominent place

A real man
With a listening heart
He makes diplomacy
Look like an art
May God bless and keep him
      Through harrowing times
His decency puts him
At the head of the line.

DEDICATIONS

This book of modern poetry is dedicated to my three loves – Denai Helene, Samantha Rae and Vincent David, the few people on this planet who were encouraging and supportive of my dream. Special thanks to my dear friend Michelle for her steadfast encouragement. Also, thank you Ed for all your help.

And this book is especially dedicated to the memory of my wonderful mother, Helena Barton.

Also to all LGBT teens and youth that struggle to become their authentic selves with the right to their own unique identities.

D.S. Barton

PEACE OUT.

CPSIA information can be obtained at www.ICGtesting.com
Printed in the USA
LVOW08*2240121214

418630LV00001B/2/P